Penny and Lars

by POMPETTE

WHITE STAR PUBLISHERS

Penny is a penguin from the South Pole.

Lars is a polar bear from the North Pole.

They come from opposite sides of the world
but they've become best friends.
This is a book about their friendship.

Daily Routine

Penny likes to get up early.

She has her breakfast and is ready for the day.

Lars likes to sleep.

He has a hard time getting up.

In the afternoon (when Lars is finally up)

they take a tea break together

and go for their daily walk.

Napping

Sometimes Penny falls asleep while waiting...

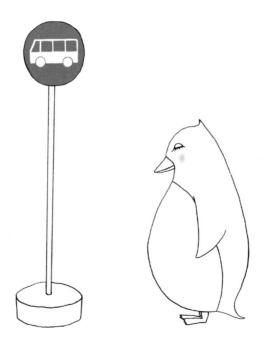

Sometimes Lars falls asleep while reading...

Sometimes they fall asleep together...

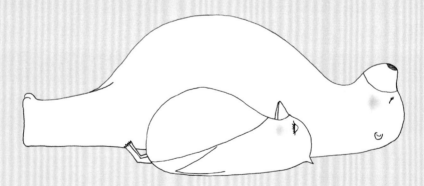

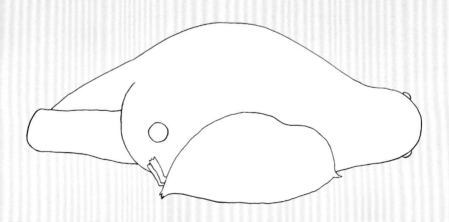

Likes and Dislikes

Penny likes fish

and Lars likes steak.

Penny doesn't like broccoli

and Lars doesn't like tomatoes.

So they trade their broccoli and tomato,

but they promise each other to at least eat one.

On a special day,
they share their favorite strawberry cake for dessert.

They both **love** cake!

Dancing

When Penny has good news,

Penny and Lars do a little dance in the garden.

When Lars has good news,

they do a little dance in the living room.

When they both have good news,

they start dancing anywhere!

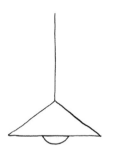

Help!

Penny needed to change the light bulb, but she couldn't reach the lamp.

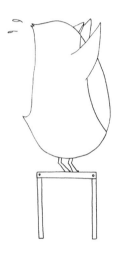

Lars was trying to assemble his new bookcase, but he got stuck...

So Penny helped Lars assemble his bookcase

and Lars helped Penny change her light bulb.

Ice Cream

Penny's favorite ice cream flavor is chocolate.

Lars' favorite ice cream flavor is vanilla.

When Penny is upset,
Lars brings her a tub of chocolate ice cream.

He knows that it will make her smile.

When Lars is feeling down,
Penny brings him a tub of vanilla ice cream.

She knows that it will make him feel better.

When they both want ice cream
they go to their favorite ice cream shop

or make sundaes at home.

Secrets

Really?

Oh-my-goodness

Weekends

Penny likes being outside.
She enjoys gardening.

Lars likes to relax indoors.
He enjoys reading.

Their weekend starts with a big stack of pancakes

and ends with a movie and a big bowl of popcorn.

Picnic

- Spring -

Penny loves cooking with herbs from her garden.

Lars is a master at baking.

When the weather is nice,

they take a big picnic basket to the park

and watch the sunset together.

At the Pool

- Summer -

Penny likes floating in the pool.

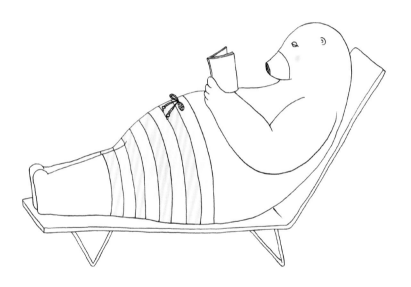

Lars likes to lay by the pool.

After a full day under the sun,

they both like to cool down with a frozen Piña Colada.

Camping

- Fall -

When Penny and Lars go camping,

Penny likes to kayak in the river

and Lars likes to explore the woods.

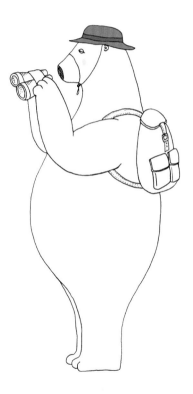

Their favorite part of camping is starting a campfire

and singing their favorite songs all night long.

Ice Fishing

- Winter -

Penny is a beginner at ice fishing,

so Lars tries to teach her some tips,

but Penny gets tired of waiting and falls asleep...

Of course, when it's time to eat the fish,

Penny is wide awake!

Getting Ready

Looking good ♡

Christmas

What did Penny get for Christmas?

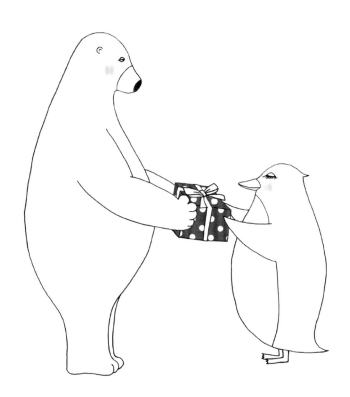

A lovely hat.

It's a little big for her, but she's excited.
She has always wanted a red hat.

What did Lars get for Christmas?

A dashing scarf.

It's a little short for him, but he's thrilled.
He looks handsome in it.

Penny and Lars are thankful for having each other
because when they're together,
ordinary things become **extraordinary**.

See you!

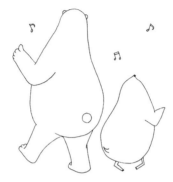

Text and illustration © 2017 Pompette
"Penny & Lars" by Pompette
Visit Penny & Lars and Pompette's other creations at:
www.be-pompette.com

WHITE STAR PUBLISHERS

© 2017 White Star s.r.l.
Piazzale Luigi Cadorna, 6 – 20123 Milan, Italy
www.whitestar.it

ISBN 978-88-544-1114-2
1 2 3 4 5 6   21 20 19 18 17

Printed in China